Bad Dad Jokes Book

ZiesMerch

With 13 bananas in one hand and 10 oranges in the other, what do you have?

Big Hands

What did the clock do when it was hungry?

It went back four seconds.

Someone stole a full case of Red Bull from my store.

I don't know how they can sleep at night.

Why did the horses get a divorce?

They didn't have a stable relationship.

Why do people rarely starve in the desert?

Because of all the sand which is there.

I stopped looking for my watch.

I just couldn't find the time.

How do you get a squirrel
to like you?

Act like a nut.

How do you make a tissue
dance?

You put a little boogie in it.

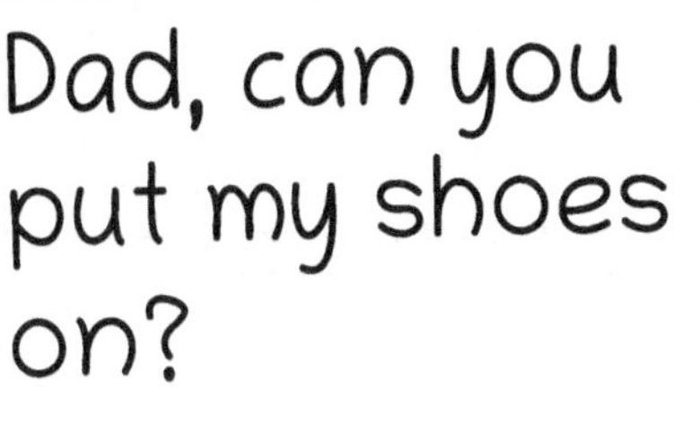

Dad, can you put my shoes on?

No, I don't think they'll fit me.

What do you call cheese that isn't yours?

Nacho cheese.

I'll never understand how people have a hard time sleeping. It's so easy, I do it with both eyes closed.

You haven't heard the joke about the three deep holes? Well, well, well.

I finally found work as a baker's assistant. I really knead the dough.

A limbo champion walked
into a bar...he was
disqualified.

One time I paid $20 to
see Prince in concert. But
I partied like its $19.99.

I accidentally glued my autobiography to my hand, but no one seems to believe me. That's my story, and I'm sticking to it.

During high school, we lived on a houseboat. I fell in love with the girl next door but eventually we drifted apart.

To whoever stole my copy of Microsoft Office, I will find you. You have my Word.

Why are mountain ranges funny?

Because they're hill areas.

Tell me one thing wrong
with overstocking grocery
shelves.

Go on. Aisle weight.

Do you know what
happened to the cocky
lion trainer at the zoo?

He was consumed by his
own pride.

I asked the store clerk
where to find the
Terminator DVDs.

He responded,
"Aisle B, back."

Did you hear about the
actor that literally broke a
leg on stage?

Don't worry; he's still in
the cast.

What's the difference between a jeweler and a jailer?

One sells watches, while the other watches cells.

I have my grandmother on speed-dial.

We call it Instagram.

What type of music do wind turbines enjoy?

They're huge metal fans.

Why couldn't Usain Bolt listen to music while running?

He kept breaking the record.

What sound does a 747
make when it bounces?

Boeing, Boeing, Boeing.

What did the right eye say
to the left eye?

Between you and me,
something smells.

I changed my iPod's name to "Titantic" in iTunes.

It's syncing now.

My job as a freight elevator repairman...has its ups and downs.

It's tricky knowing when to take the tea bag out. There's a steep learning curve.

Ladies, if he can't appreciate your fruit jokes, you need to let the mango.

I went into a pet shop and said: "I would like a pet parrot for my daughter." Confused, the owner replied: "Sorry, we don't do swaps."

If your parachute doesn't deploy...you have the rest of your life to fix it.

Why did Stalin only write
in lowercase?

He didn't like capitalism.

Do you know what
happened to the turkey?
He didn't Czech his flight
plans and ended up in
Greece. People were
Hungary.

I was offered a job as an undertaker but I turned it down.

I couldn't dig it.

I don't trust stairs. They're always up to something.

I've got a great joke about construction, but I'm still working on it.

You know, people say they pick their nose, but I feel like I was just born with mine.

I made a pencil with two erasers. It was pointless.

What do you get from a pampered cow?

Spoiled milk.

It takes guts to be an organ donor.

Can February March? No, but April May!

When does a joke become
a dad joke?

When it becomes
apparent.

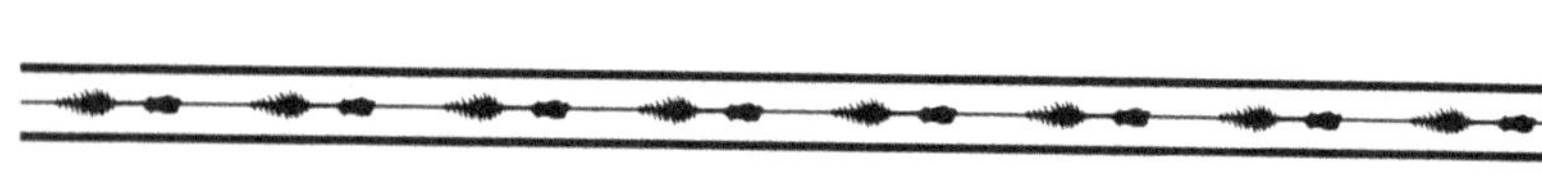

Did you hear about the
guy who invented the
knock-knock joke?

He won the 'no-bell' prize.

I wanted to go on a diet,
but I feel like I have way
too much on my plate right
now.

I tell dad jokes, but I don't
have any kids. I'm a faux
pa.

What do you call a bear
without any teeth?

A gummy bear!

Dad, can you put the cat
out? I didn't know it was
on fire.

How do you make holy water?

You boil the hell out of it.

Dad, did you get a haircut?
No, I got them all cut.

Why couldn't the bicycle stand up by itself?

It was two tired.

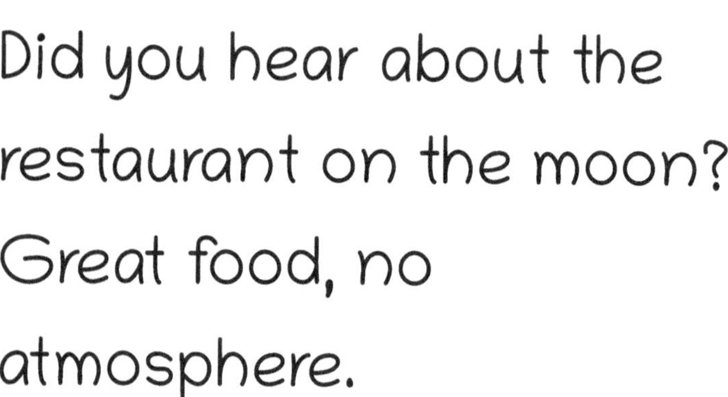

Did you hear about the restaurant on the moon?

Great food, no atmosphere.

What do you call a man
with a rubber toe?
Roberto.

Why was the belt sent to
jail?

For holding up a pair of
pants!

What's an astronaut's favorite part of a computer?

The space bar.

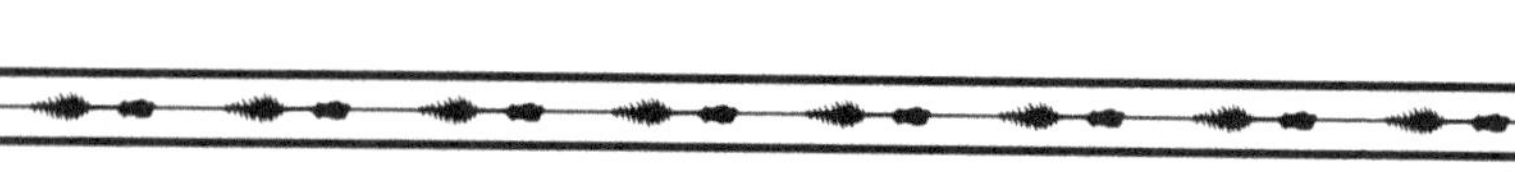

Do you think glass coffins will be a success?
Remains to be seen.

What do you call a baby
monkey?

A chimp off the old block.

What lies at the bottom of
the ocean and twitches?

A nervous wreck.

Two cannibals are eating a clown. One says to the other: "Does this taste funny to you?"

What happens when a frogs car dies?

He needs a jump. If that doesn't work he has to get it toad.

What time did the man go to the dentist?

Tooth hurt-y!

Does anyone need an ark?

I Noah guy!

What do you call a fish
with two knees?

A two-knee fish!

Why did the coffee file a
police report?

It got mugged.

What do you call someone with no body and no nose?

Nobody knows.

Did you know the first French fries weren't actually cooked in France? They were cooked in Greece.

What is the least spoken language in the world?

Sign language.

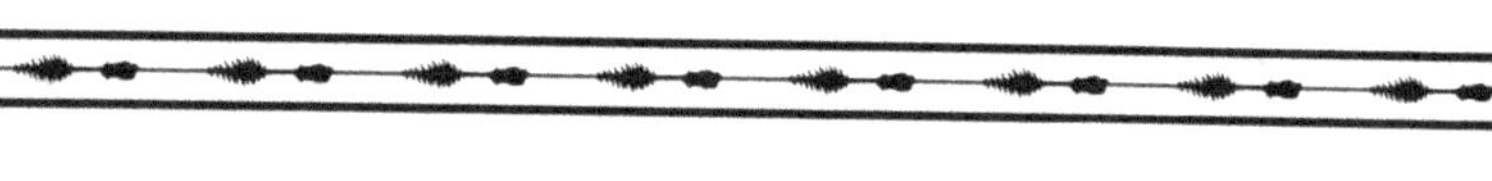

If you see a robbery at an Apple Store does that make you an iWitness?

Why did the invisible man turn down the job offer?

He couldn't see himself doing it.

A slice of apple pie is $2.50 in Jamaica and $3.00 in the Bahamas. These are the pie rates of the Caribbean.

What did the buffalo say to his son when he dropped him off at school?

Bison.

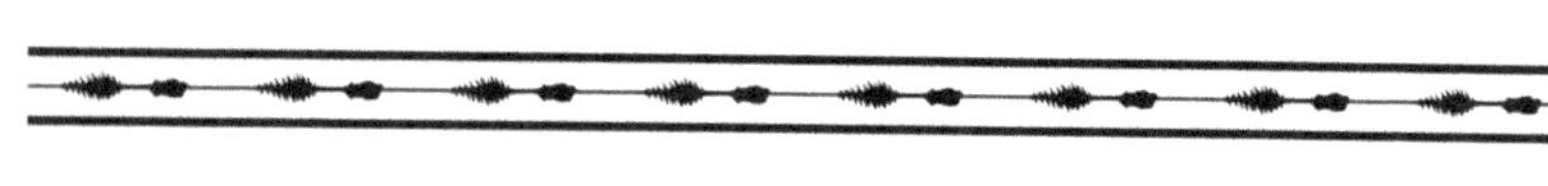

You know what the loudest pet you can get is?

A trumpet.

Why did the crab never share?

Because he's shellfish.

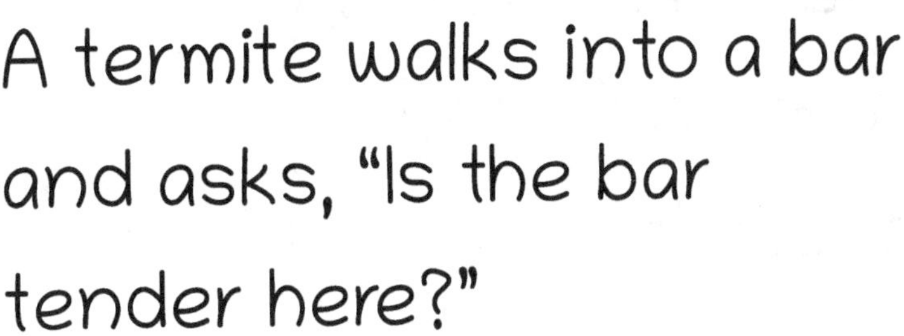

A termite walks into a bar and asks, "Is the bar tender here?"

I'm only familiar with 25 letters in the English language. I don't know why.

I hear it's easy to get ladies not to eat Tide pods. It's more difficult to deter gents, though.

Don't trust atoms. They make up everything!

Mom: "How do I look?"

Dad: "With your eyes."

What do you call a man who can't stand? Neil.

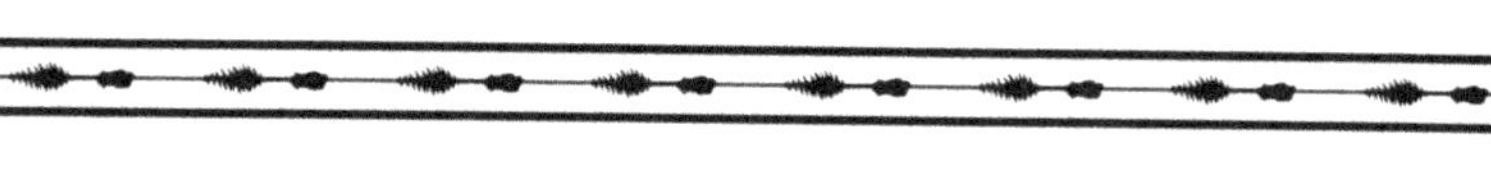

Why did the picture go to jail?

Because it was framed.

Did you hear about the circus fire?

It was in tents.

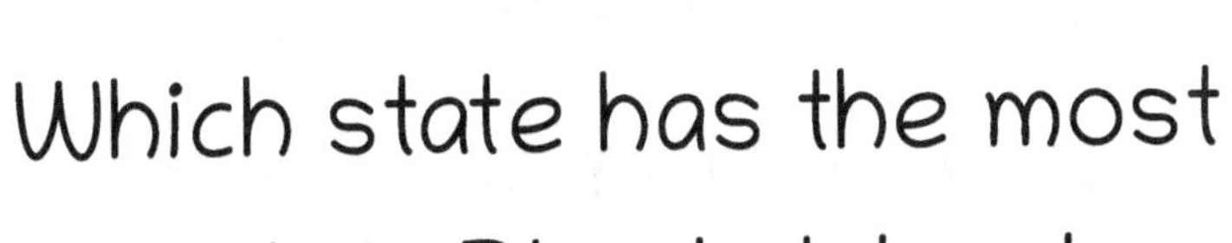

Which state has the most streets? Rhode Island.

Why do chicken coops only have two doors? Because if they had four, they'd be chicken sedans.

What do you get when you cross a snowman with a vampire? Frostbite.

I'm reading a book about zero gravity chambers... I can't put it down.

When shopping for a vacuum cleaner, check the reviews. Pick the one that sucks the most.

My uncle stores his coin collection in Altoids tins. He claims it keeps them in mint condition.

What do you call a four foot six psychic that escaped from prison?

A small medium at large.

I have this terrible condition where I'm only happy waiting in airports. My doctor says it's terminal.

Did you hear the news about the shovel? It's ground breaking. But the broom? That really swept the nation.

My girlfriend poked me in the eyes. I stopped seeing her for a little while.

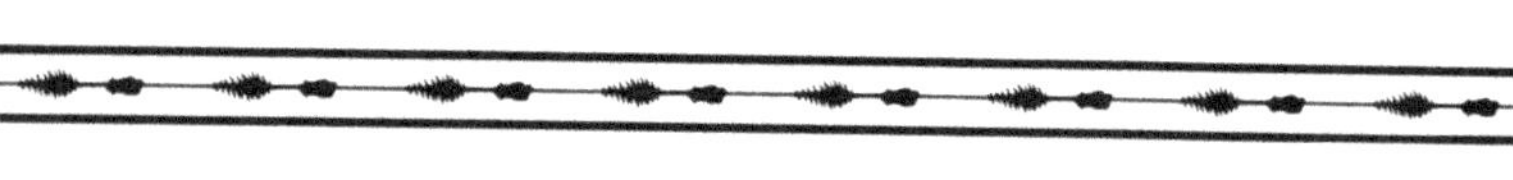

Mark Hamill made a lot of money for his role as Skywalker in Star Wars. One might say it was Lucrative.

What do you call a cow
with no legs?

Ground beef.

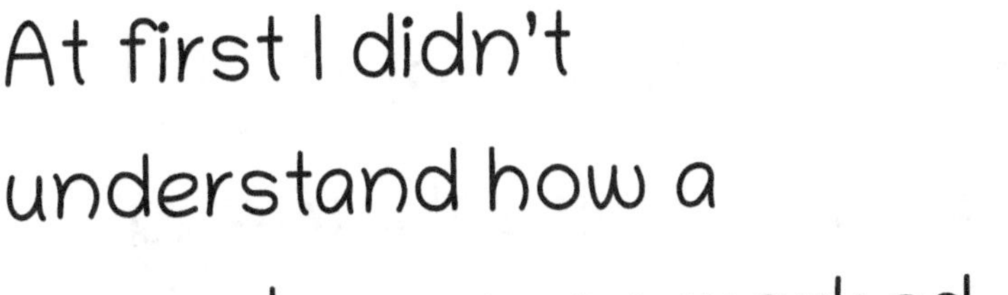

At first I didn't
understand how a
computer mouse worked.
But then it just clicked.

You want to know the way
to my heart?

A scalpel and a bone saw.

How do rhinos and
elephants like their eggs?

Any way but poached.

What do sprinters eat
before a race?

Nothing, they fast!

What concert costs just
45 cents?

50 Cent featuring
Nickelback!

Why did the scarecrow win an award?

Because he was outstanding in his field!

What do you call a mac 'n' cheese that gets all up in your face?

Too close for comfort food!

What happens when you go to the bathroom in France? European.

Why do melons have weddings?

Because they cantaloupe!

What's the difference between a poorly dressed man on a tricycle and a well-dressed man on a bicycle? Attire!

Did you hear the rumor about butter?

Well, I'm not going to spread it!

How many apples grow on a tree?

All of them!

Why don't skeletons ever go trick or treating?
Because they have no body to go with!

Did you hear about the Italian chef who died?

He pasta way!

When the grocery store clerk asks me if I want the milk in a bag, I always tell him, "No, I'd rather drink it out of the carton!"

What's ET short for?

Because he's only got tiny legs!

What's orange and sounds like a parrot?

A carrot!

I invented a new word
today: Plagiarism!

After dinner, my wife
asked if I could clear the
table. I needed a running
start, but I made it!

Why is Peter Pan always flying?

He neverlands!

A woman is on trial for beating her husband to death with his guitar collection. The judge asks her, "First offender?" She says, "No, first a Gibson! Then a Fender!"

I know a lot of jokes about retired people but none of them work!

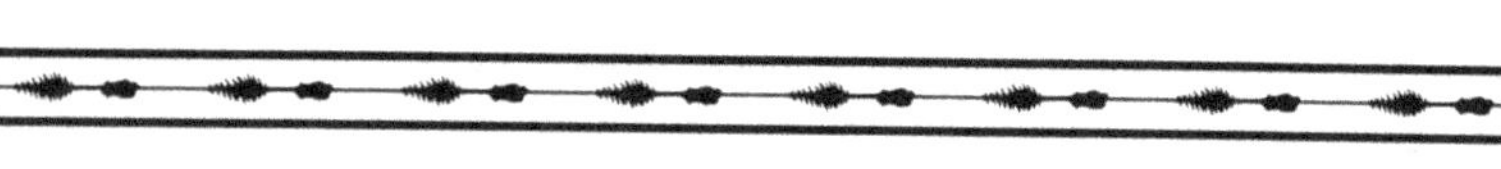

What do Santa's elves listen to ask they work? Wrap music!

How does a penguin build
its house?

Igloos it together!

What do you call a factory
that sells passable
products?

A satisfactory!

I used to work in a shoe-recycling shop. It was sole destroying!

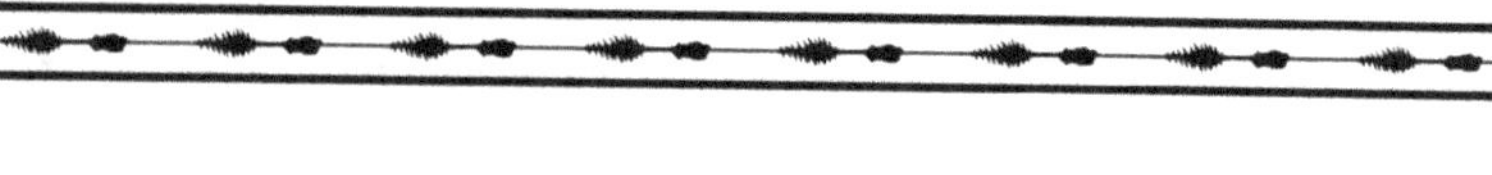

Spring is here! I got so excited I wet my plants!

My friend says to me, "What rhymes with orange?"

And I told him, "No it doesn't!"

My wife told me I had to stop acting like a flamingo. So I had to put my foot down!

My uncle named his dogs
Rolex and Timex. They're
his watch dogs!

Five out of four people
admit they're bad with
fractions!

Two goldfish are in a tank. One says to the other, "Do you know how to drive this thing?"

I'll call you later. Don't call me later, call me Dad!

If an English teacher is convicted of a crime and doesn't complete the sentence, is that a fragment?

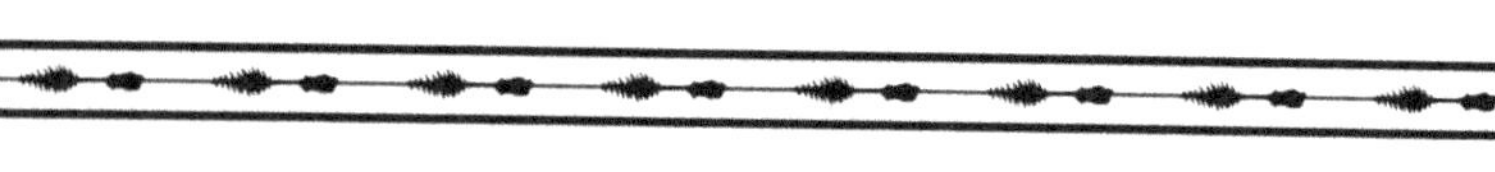

Which U.S. state is famous for its extra-small soft drinks?

Minnesota!

What did the Ranch say when someone opened the refrigerator door?

"Close the door, I'm dressing!"

Why do trees seem suspicious on sunny days?

They just seem a little shady!

What did the policeman say to his belly button?

You're under a vest!

A cheese factory exploded in France. Da brie is everywhere!

What do you give to a sick lemon?

Lemon aid!

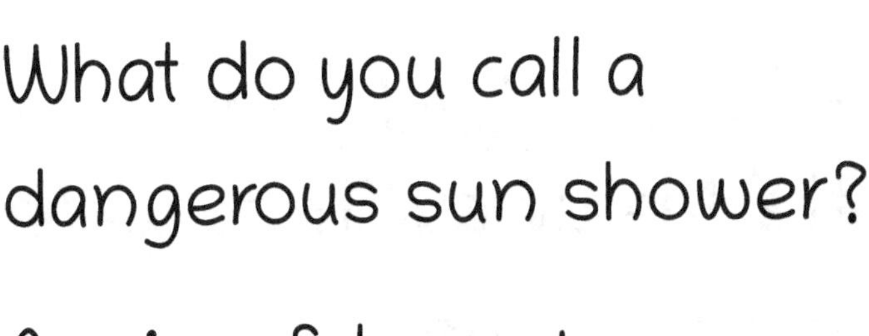

What do you call a dangerous sun shower?

A rain of terror!

What do you call birds who stick together?

Vel-crows.

Today I gave my dead batteries away. They were free of charge.

I went on a once-in-a-lifetime vacation. Never again.

Thank you for purchasing this book. I hope you groaned, sighed and laughed your way through it.

www.ingramcontent.com/pod-product-compliance
Lightning Source LLC
Chambersburg PA
CBHW072120150726
47999CB00005B/2059